Piano
Preludes

by
Michael Valenti

Associated Music Publishers, Inc.

DISTRIBUTED BY

HAL•LEONARD®
CORPORATION

7777 W. BLUEMOUND RD. P.O. BOX 13819 MILWAUKEE, WI 53213

Copyright © 1974, 1980 Associated Music Publishers, Inc., New York
All Rights Reserved   International Copyright Secured   Printed in U.S.A.
No part of this work may be reproduced or transmitted in any form or by any means, electronic or mechanical, including photocopying or by any information storage and retrieval system, without permission in writing from the publisher.

To Steven A. Martindale

PIANO PRELUDES

1.

(ROCKTATA)

Michael Valenti

Copyright © 1974 Associated Music Publishers, Inc., New York
All Rights Reserved   International Copyright Secured   Printed in U.S.A.
This work may not be reproduced in whole or in part by any means, electronic or mechanical, including photocopying, without permission in writing from the publishers.

5

2.

Michael Valenti

Moderato ma non troppo

Copyright © 1980 Associated Music Publishers, Inc., New York
All Rights Reserved   International Copyright Secured   Printed in U.S.A.
This work may not be reproduced in whole or in part by any means, electronic or me
chanical, including photocopying, without permission in writing from the publishers.

poco rall.

3.

Michael Valenti

Allegretto

Copyright © 1980 Associated Music Publishers, Inc., New York
All Rights Reserved   International Copyright Secured   Printed in U.S.A.
This work may not be reproduced in whole or in part by any means, electronic or me-
chanical, including photocopying, without permission in writing from the publishers.

4.

Michael Valenti

Copyright © 1980 Associated Music Publishers, Inc., New York
All Rights Reserved   International Copyright Secured   Printed in U.S.A.
This work may not be reproduced in whole or in part by any means, electronic or me-
chanical, including photocopying, without permission in writing from the publishers.

5.

Michael Valenti

Copyright © 1980 Associated Music Publishers, Inc., New York
All Rights Reserved   International Copyright Secured   Printed in U.S.A.
This work may not be reproduced in whole or in part by any means, electronic or me-
chanical, including photocopying, without permission in writing from the publishers.

14

6.

Michael Valenti

Moderato

Copyright © 1980 Associated Music Publishers, Inc., New York
All Rights Reserved   International Copyright Secured   Printed in U.S.A.
This work may not be reproduced in whole or in part by any means, electronic or me-
chanical, including photocopying, without permission in writing from the publishers.

7.

Michael Valenti

Copyright © 1980 Associated Music Publishers, Inc., New York
All Rights Reserved   International Copyright Secured   Printed in U.S.A.
This work may not be reproduced in whole or in part by any means, electronic or me-
chanical, including photocopying, without permission in writing from the publishers.

8.

Michael Valenti

Adagietto
con dolore
p legato
simile

1. poco rall. Tempo I
p L. H.

2. rall. ritard.
pp

Copyright © 1980 Associated Music Publishers, Inc., New York
All Rights Reserved   International Copyright Secured   Printed in U.S.A.
This work may not be reproduced in whole or in part by any means, electronic or me-
chanical, including photocopying, without permission in writing from the publishers.

9.

Rubato

Michael Valenti

Copyright © 1980 Associated Music Publishers, Inc., New York
All Rights Reserved   International Copyright Secured   Printed in U.S.A.
This work may not be reproduced in whole or in part by any means, electronic or me-
chanical, including photocopying, without permission in writing from the publishers.

10.

Michael Valenti

Copyright © 1980 Associated Music Publishers, Inc., New York
All Rights Reserved   International Copyright Secured   Printed in U.S.A.
This work may not be reproduced in whole or in part by any means, electronic or me-
chanical, including photocopying, without permission in writing from the publishers.

L'istesso tempo

24

L'istesso tempo

11.

Michael Valenti

Copyright © 1980 Associated Music Publishers, Inc., New York
All Rights Reserved   International Copyright Secured   Printed in U.S.A.
This work may not be reproduced in whole or in part by any means, electronic or me-
chanical, including photocopying, without permission in writing from the publishers.

12.

Michael Valenti

Copyright © 1980 Associated Music Publishers, Inc., New York
All Rights Reserved   International Copyright Secured   Printed in U.S.A.
This work may not be reproduced in whole or in part by any means, electronic or me-
chanical, including photocopying, without permission in writing from the publishers.

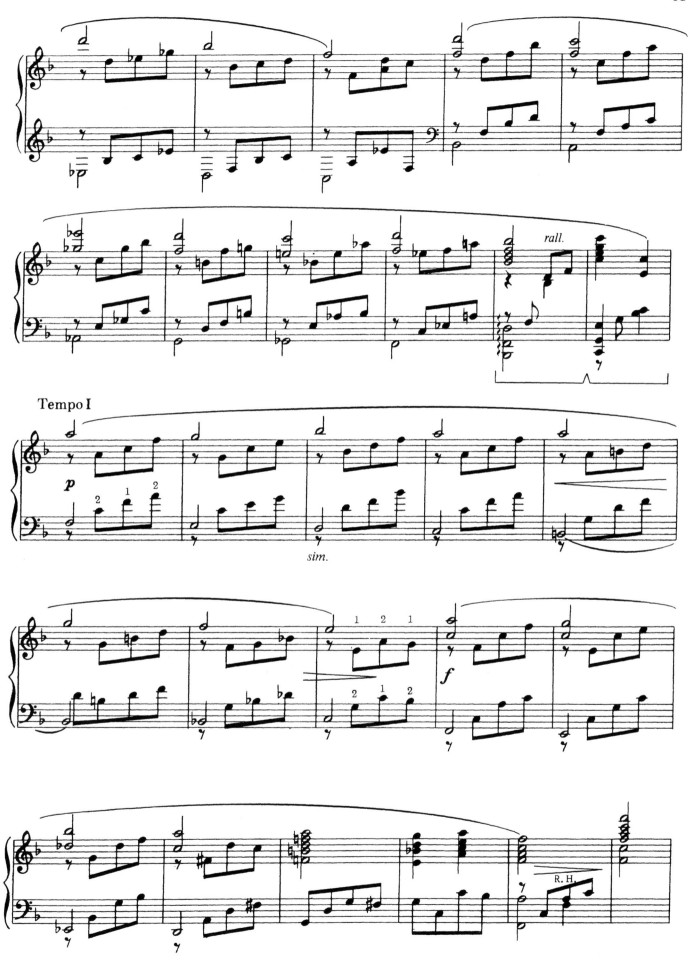

New York, 1979